"Opportunity knocking? Can you hold?"

THE LOAN BARN
BINGE BORROWERS WELCOME!
MANKOFF 12E

"Look this over—it's a plan to balance our checkbook by 1991."

"Son, we Billinghams have always made our careers in medicine, law or finance—that's why I want you to reconsider your plan to become a Mafia don."

"According to our lie detector test, drug test, psychological test and intelligence test, you're honest, drug free, mentally stable and dumb."

"He's young—I don't like that in a man."

"No, you're not boring me—I'm a tax-code freak."

"All those in favor say 'Aye,' all those out of favor, leave."

"Help! I'm trapped in middle management!"

Let's face it, Mr. Bidner. In your price range you can't afford to have a city apartment and claustrophobia."

"Miss Demby, bring in my rose-colored glasses. I don't like the looks of this projection."

"Amazing, eh? But believe me, every word of that resume is based on a true story."

"And you, Russ, if you were stranded on a desert island, what financial newsletter would you want?"

"Watch your back, guys—this is the fast track."

"Oh, hiring's all right, but I think my real calling is firing."

"So, how many brands of birds do they make?"

"I used to write the songs—now I write the insurance policies."

"I've got nothing against honesty, but scrupulous honesty gets on my nerves."

"Long-term, I like bonds; intermediate-term, I like equities; and short-term, I like scotch."

"Neither a borrower nor a lender be."

"What do you want to work on tonight—our relationship or our taxes?"

"Dorothy, Mr. Zwerdling won't be in today—here's a list of the people he wants sacked."

"Now, do any of you other yes-men have a 'yes, but' you'd like to get off your chest?"

"Gentlemen, start your engines."

ORGANIZATION CHART
MANKOFF

"Teddy, we're thinking of making you a partner, but, for reasons I don't think I have to elaborate, we'd like you to change your name from Ruxpin."

"I think you two will enjoy each other immensely. However, I am in no way liable for any pain, suffering, loss or damage caused by, or alleged to result from, this introduction."

"I thought it was a myth, but it's true—when you're fired, your whole resume flashes before your eyes."

"Look, just finish college, get your MBA, have a career, retire, and then if you want to try your hand at acting, you'll have my blessing."

"I'm a great believer in keeping a clean desk, chief."

"I'm really quite comfortable with failure on this level."

I was a late bloomer—I didn't inherit my money until my fifties."

"What do you say we let the service sector handle our dining needs for tonight?"

"I make no apologies for my wealth, Dan, I pay people to do that."

"Supermom isn't home right now—she's out fighting for truth, justice and a buck."

"Adorable, but we don't take children as collateral."

"Didn't you ever have a book you just couldn't put down?"

"By the way, I've ordered a new set of worldly possessions."

"Mr. Dankin, the plumber will see you now."

I ♥ $

"Get me the Coast."

"Here it is, previously unavailable for purchase at any price, now yours for only $39.95!"

"Hodgkins, if it's not too much trouble we'd like you to take your vacation in the office this year."

THREE CHEERS FOR ADVERTISING

SECURO
ARMORED CAR CO.
BUCKS ON BOARD
MANKOFF

"No, I don't find it boring here, I was an accountant."

"No kidding? My late husband was in organized crime."

NOBODY HAS GOTTEN BACK TO ME IN TWO YEARS.

TIME TO RETIRE

MANKOFF

MANKOFF 78

"Repeat that offer in a business setting . . . party talk is cheap."

"I'm an idealist—I'd like to make my pile at a non-profit organization."

"OK, let's go to contract."

"Pack your bags, Vinnie . . . this is a Burger King town."

"Oh, I've been a rich man, a poor man, a beggar man, a thief, a doctor, a lawyer and now I'd like to try my hand at heading a native-American tribal organization."

"Well, should we need any more useless and unproductive employees who are a burden to the organization we'll be sure to give you a call, Mr. Deadwood."

"Welcome aboard, and, if you have any problem at all, don't hesitate to shut up."

"I know it's a crucial time for the company, sir, but I've got to go down to the sea again."

"I'm flexible—I want to be rich and famous, but I'll settle for rich."

"Could we talk about something else? Business is so boring."

"Look, I'm only doing this because begging and borrowing haven't worked for me."

"Well, you may be right about the economy, but I'll be damned if I'll agree with anybody who has a tiny umbrella in his drink."

"This is my lawyer—he's going to handle the fine print."

"They've been hard times, Al, but they've been fun times, too."

"Corporate raiders, sir . . . one, maybe two companies away."

"Sure you'll be cramped, but you'll be cramped in luxury."

"So, in a nutshell, quality of life insurance protects you and your family in the event of the death of your life style."

"It comes with everything you see on the sticker . . . except the radio, which has already been stolen."

DECISIONS, DECISIONS

HONEST ABIE'S APPLIANCES

STAYING IN BUSINESS!

WE HAVEN'T LOST OUR LEASE!

PRICES ABOUT THE SAME AS ELSEWHERE!

MANKOFF 98

"It's a little bit small, but it's got great cross ventilation."

"Right now we're very bullish on Girl Scout cookies."

"I'd like to stay, sir, but time is running out if I want to start a rock group."

"You know, Tom, aside from huge amounts of money, my wants are very few."

THIRTY DAYS TO A FATTER WALLET
MANKOFF 96

THE SENSUOUS ACCOUNTANT
MANKOFF

"Did you ever have one of those days when the profit motive just wasn't motive enough?"

"Who would have thought that when I asked you to have your people talk to my people they'd realize we were superfluous."

"What do you mean, 'Have your lawyer call my lawyer'? . . . you are my lawyer!"

"I've got franks, knishes, hot pretzels and a full range of financial services."

"And in the heart you want 'Bertie loves Turnbull, Behan, Tagley & Fisk'?"

CALIFORNIA ENTREPRENEUR

FALL
FOLIAGE

"Oh, I know the CEO position around here is out, but as far as I'm concerned everything else is up for grabs."

HAMLET FOR THE EIGHTIES

"I got a second opinion on the operation—my accountant advises against it."

"Look, Miss Knepper, we're working your money as hard as possible, but right now your money is just pooped."

"But will monetary policies introduced to stabilize growth actually lead to a more volatile economy in the long run? Well, that's a subject for another party."

"That's what I like about you, Eddie . . . scientists may need a $6 billion atom smasher to explore the fundamental questions of nature, but all you need is one too many."

CASH
BINGO!
MANKOFF

"No, stay!"

"Let me put it this way—I am to stocks and bonds as David Byrne is to rock and roll."

"Sir, how can I take your criticism of me seriously when I'm my own worst critic and I think I'm doing such a great job?"

"Up to my floor and then right down again, Eddie . . . I'm just going through the motions today."

BOWTHER
WILKIN
LYNCH
&
FISK
MANKOFF
12B

DESKS
MANKOFF

CORPORATE LADDER

MANKOFF

"C'mon—I'm telling you there's money in land."

"Tell me more about your feeling toward the parent company."

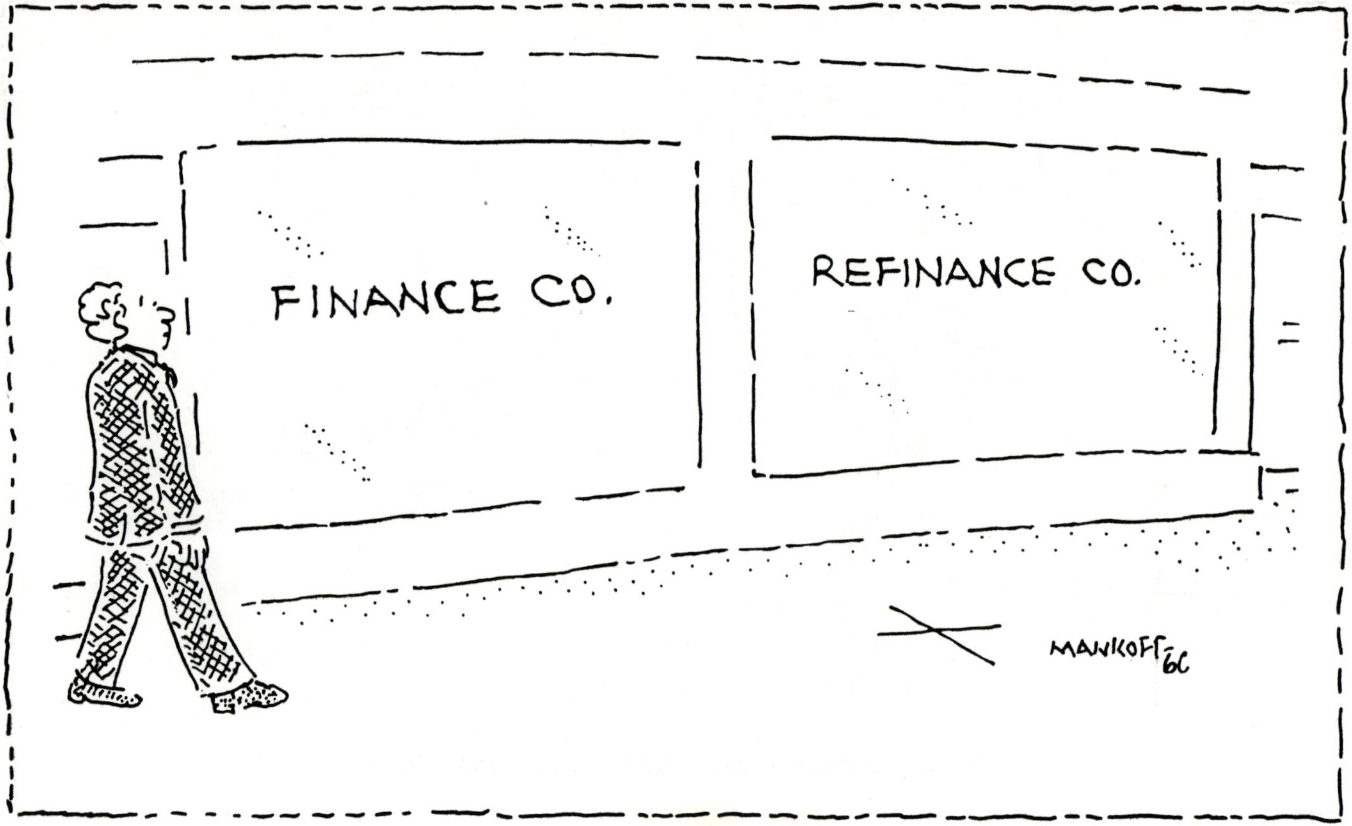

FINANCE CO.

REFINANCE CO.

MANKOFF 86

"Buddy Krell—bail bondsman to the stars."

THE OPTIMIST
ENTER HERE
MANKOFF

"I still can't believe you're leaving a two bedroom for a studio."

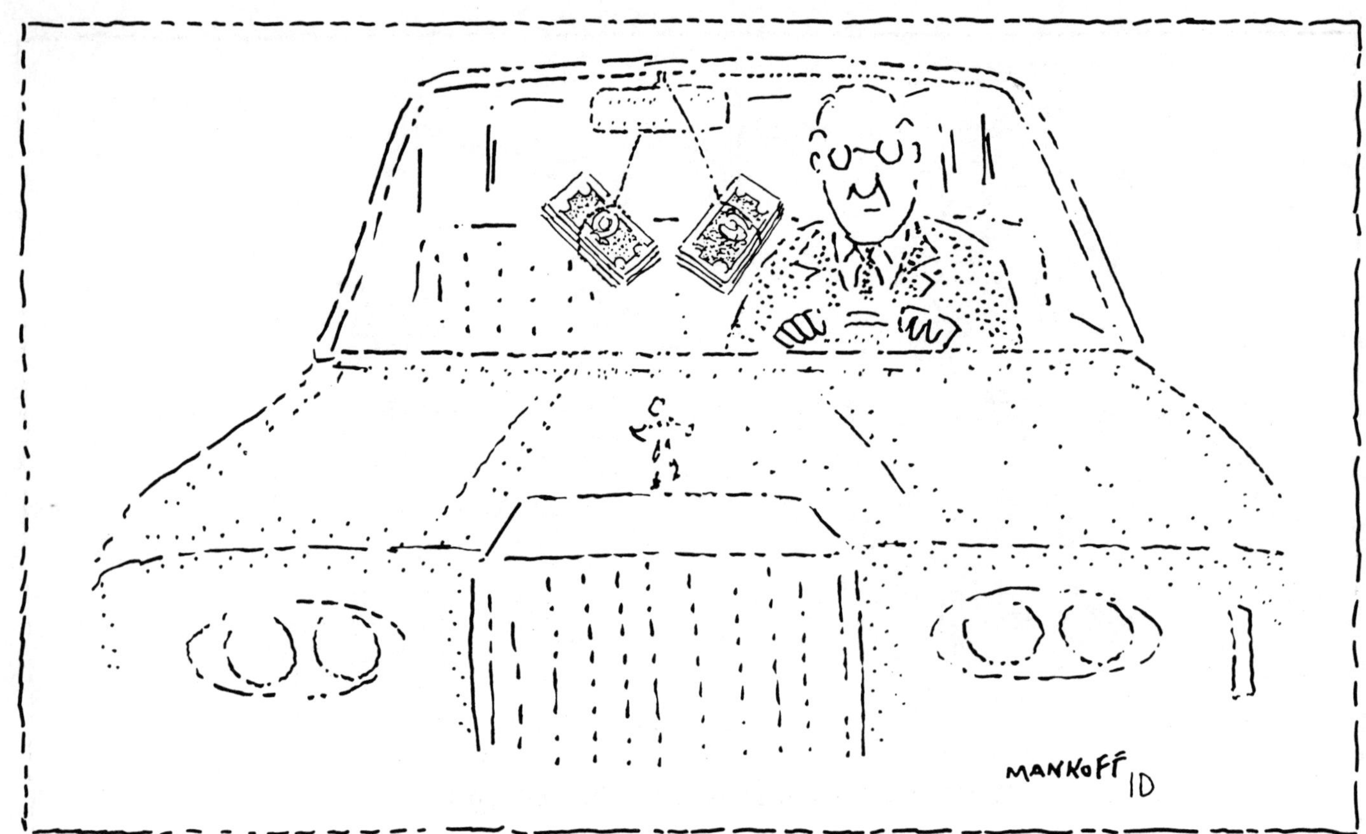
MANKOFF
ID

"I'd like some means to achieve my ends."

BURGLAR
MOVING CO.
MANKOFF

"I probably sound pretty stupid here, but, believe me, in a business setting with lots of underlings nodding in agreement, I'm very persuasive."

"Yes, son, we are the idle rich . . . but our money works overtime."

"Oh, he's more than my significant other—he's my co-mortgagor."

"What do you say we just call it a failed joint venture?"

UNHYPED
HYPED
OVERHYPED
DEHYPED
MANKOFF

FORGOT
WHICH SIDE
MY BREAD
WAS
BUTTERED ON
MANKOFF

"Could you handle this . . . I'm all decisioned-out for today."

"A motion to democratize the board has been made and quashed."

NO
RADIO
MANKOFF

"Hi, I'm the new you."

"B.J. has a 'hands-on' management style."

"Hey, I just consider myself very fortunate to be getting paid for something I'd be doing anyway."

I'VE LOOKED AT OPTIONS TRADING
FROM BOTH SIDES NOW,
FROM WIN AND LOSE
AND STILL SOME HOW,
IT'S OPTIONS TRADINGS ILLUSIONS
I RECALL,
I GUESS I DON'T KNOW
OPTIONS TRADINGS AT ALL.
MANKOFF

"There, there, have yourself a good cry and then clear out."

"Good news, Davey, the studio has decided to option your memo."

"This suit says, 'I'm a man on the way up.'"

"Summertime, chief, and the livin' is easy."

"Bad news, we've been kicked out of the middle class."

DANGER
FALLING
DOLLAR

"Here's the dough—and remember the collateral is your knees."

WALL STREET
CLINIC FOR THE MORALLY DISABLED

MANKOFF 68